Table of Contents

Grandparents' Day - First Sunday after Labor Day

Bear Hug Card

Materials:

- pattern for bear template (page 3) cut from tagboard
- bear card patterns (page 4)
- 9" x 12" (23 x 30.5 cm) brown construction paper
- crayons or felt pens; scissors; glue

Steps to follow:

1. Lay the bear template on brown construction paper. Trace around the template, and then cut out the bear.

2. Fold the arms as indicated.

3. Color and cut out the bear's face and paws and either the flower or heart. Glue to the brown construction paper as shown.

4. Cut out the poem. Glue it inside the card on the bear's tummy.

Optional:

Have students write original poems or other messages to go inside the bear card.

         How to Make Greeting Cards with Children • EMC 231

Pattern for bear template

       How to Make Greeting Cards with Children • EMC 231

Patterns for bear card

On this special day
that's just for you
Bear's bringing you hugs
and my love too!

Secrets

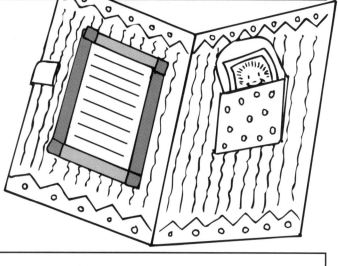

Materials:

- patterns (page 6)
- 9" x 12" (23 x 30.5 cm) white construction paper
- scraps of construction paper in bright colors
- surprise to go in pouch— memento, child's picture, message
- felt pens; scissors; glue

Steps to follow:

1. Create a pattern all over one side of the white construction paper. Design suggestions: stripes, polka dots, waves, zig-zag lines, stars.

2. Fold the paper in half with the design inside.

3. Cut out the pouch pattern. Fold and glue the pouch. Decorate it with a contrasting pattern.

4. Cut out and complete the writing form. Write a descriptive paragraph or riddle about the card's "sender."

5. Glue the writing form and the pouch inside the card.

6. Glue strips of construction paper around the writing form to create a frame. Close the card.

7. Glue a construction paper strip to the front of the card to add color. Use a paper strip in a contrasting color as a latch to close the card.

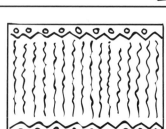

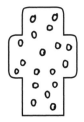

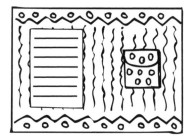

Patterns for pouch and writing form

fold

fold

fold

fold

Can you guess who thinks you are a special Grandparent?

Fill the Frame

Materials:

- patterns (page 8)
- 6" x 18" (15 x 45 cm) construction paper—any color
- ruler and pencil
- crayons; scissors; glue

Steps to follow:

1. Use the ruler to divide the construction paper into thirds (three 6" [15 cm] sections). Fold along these lines.

2. Draw a diagonal line on the front section. Cut on this line.

3. Cut out the frame pattern and writing form. Draw grandparents in the frame. Write a message on the writing form.

4. Open the construction paper and paste the frame and message inside.

5. Refold the card. Color and cut out one of the seal patterns. Glue the seal to the card to secure it.

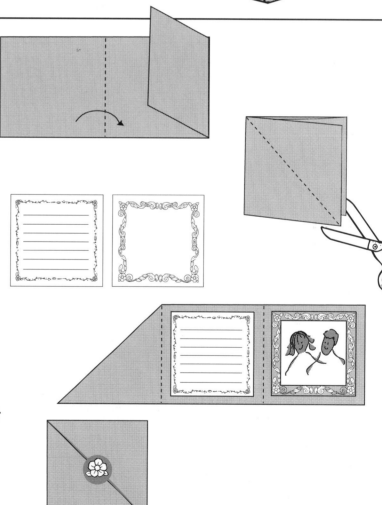

Optional:

Use a pencil eraser dipped in tempera to create a border of dots around the outside of the folded card.

Patterns for frame, greeting form, and seal

P o p - U p   T u r k e y

Materials:

- pattern (page 10)
- 9" x 12" (23 x 30.5) colored construction paper
- crayons; scissors; glue

Steps to follow:

1. Color the turkey pattern. Add feathers by tracing around fingers.

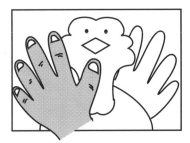

2. Fold and cut the pop-up pattern.

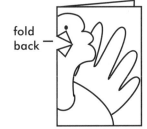

cut —   fold back —

open and pull inside

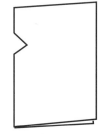

close and press folds firmly

3. Glue the pop-up inside the construction paper cover.

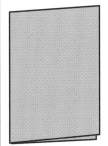 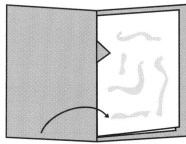

fold construction paper

Lay pop-up pattern in the cover.

Put glue on pop-up, close cover, and press. Repeat on other side of card.

4. Close the card and seal with a sticker or a paper-strip tab.

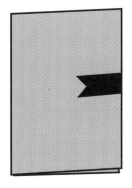

Optional:

Instead of tracing around fingers, cut or tear feathers from construction paper scraps. Glue around the turkey to form the tail.

       How to Make Greeting Cards with Children • EMC 231

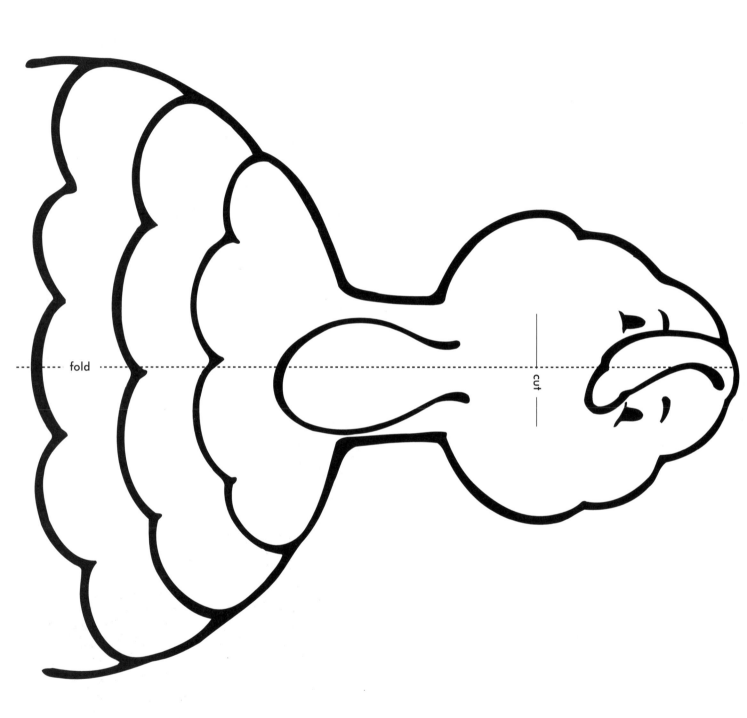

fold

cut

Thanksgiving Greeting

Materials:

- 6" x 8" (15 x 20 cm) orange construction paper
- 3 1/2" x 5 1/2" (9 x 14 cm) white construction paper
- black tempera paint (add a few drops of liquid detergent)
- paint brush
- crayons—orange, yellow, red, brown
- paper clip (unbend)
- marking pens; glue

Steps to follow:

1. Cover the entire white construction paper with spots of autumn colors. Press hard to get a thick layer of crayon. It helps to put a pad of newspaper underneath the paper.

2. Cover the crayon with a layer of black tempera. Let the paint dry completely before doing the next step.

3. Sketch the outline of several leaves in the black paint with the end of the paper clip. Then scratch out the black paint inside the leaf outlines so the autumn colors show through. (Don't press so hard the white paper shows.)

4. Fold the orange construction paper in half. Glue the leaf picture to the front of the card.

5. Write a Thanksgiving greeting or poem inside the card with marking pens.

Optional:

Scratch out a cornucopia and/or harvest fruits and vegetables.

Seven Principles Card

Materials:

- patterns (page 13) reproduced on red construction paper
- 5" x 18" (13 x 45.5 cm) black construction paper
- 1 1/2" x 18" (4 x 45.5 cm) green construction paper
- ruler and pencil
- white tempera paint; paint brush; scissors; glue

Steps to follow:

1. Fold the black construction paper as shown.

a. fold in half   b. fold back 1" (2.5 cm)

c. turn over fold back 1" (2.5 cm)

d. turn over again and repeat steps b and c

2. Cut out the pattern pieces. Glue the strips to the "mountain peaks" on the accordion folds. Glue the last strip on the right-hand side of the card.

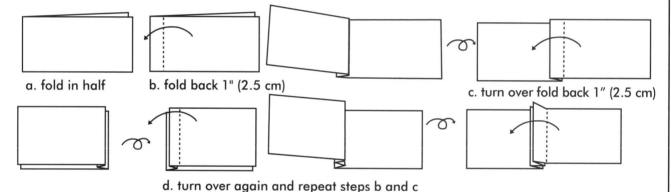

3. Paint a greeting with white paint on the left-hand side of the card.

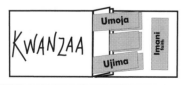

4. Close the card. Wrap the green paper strip around the card and tape closed. Glue the red seal over the taped area.

Optional:

Make paper candles instead of the principle strips. You will need 3 red, 1 black, and 3 green candles.

Patterns for principle tags and seal

Day 1 **Umoja** **Unity**	Day 2 **Kujichagulia** **self-determination**
Day 3 **Ujima** **collective work and responsibility**	Day 4 **Ujamaa** **cooperative economics**
Day 5 **Nia** **purpose**	Day 6 **Kuumba** **creativity**
Day 7 **Imani** **faith**	

- -

Day 1 **Umoja** **Unity**	Day 2 **Kujichagulia** **self-determination**
Day 3 **Ujima** **collective work and responsibility**	Day 4 **Ujamaa** **cooperative economics**
Day 5 **Nia** **purpose**	Day 6 **Kuumba** **creativity**
Day 7 **Imani** **faith**	

Pop-Up Menorah

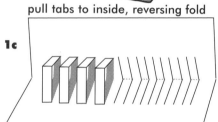

Materials:

- pattern (page 15)
- 9" x 12" (23 x 30.5 cm) blue construction paper
- 1" x 12" (2.5 x 20.5 cm) yellow construction paper
- glitter
- crayons, scissors, glue

Steps to follow:

1. Create a menorah from the pop-up pattern.

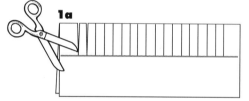

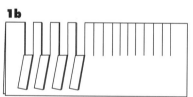

pull tabs to inside, reversing fold

2. Fold blue construction paper in half lengthwise. Glue one side of the pop-up into the construction paper. Then flip the folder over and apply glue to the other side of the pop-up. Close the folder and press firmly.

3. Cut a 3" (7.5 cm) piece off yellow strip. Use it to close the finished card. Divide remaining piece into nine 1" (2.5 cm) pieces. Cut one flame from each piece. Glue to the tip of each candle.

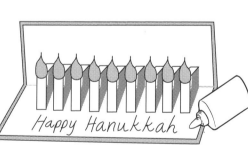

4. Outline the word Hanukkah with white glue from a squeeze bottle. Sprinkle with glitter. Allow this to dry completely before closing the card.

5. Close the card and secure with the yellow construction paper strip.

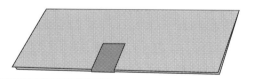

Optional:

Apply glitter to the tips of the candles for added sparkle.

Use colored pencils or marking pens to add a simple border to the outside of the greeting card.

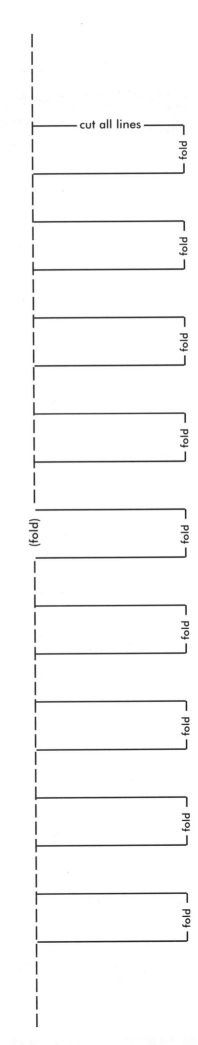

Hanging Dreidel Greeting

Materials:

- patterns (page 17)
- 20" (51 cm) yarn or string
- paste
- crayons; scissors

Steps to follow:

1. Color and cut out the four dreidel patterns. Fold each piece in half along the line.

2. Paste the folded dreidels back-to-back as shown. Leave the last section open.

3. Fold the string in half. Paste the string inside the last section. Glue the last section closed.

4. Fold the "Happy Hanukkah" card in half. Punch a hole as shown.

5. Run one end of the string through the hole and knot the other end.

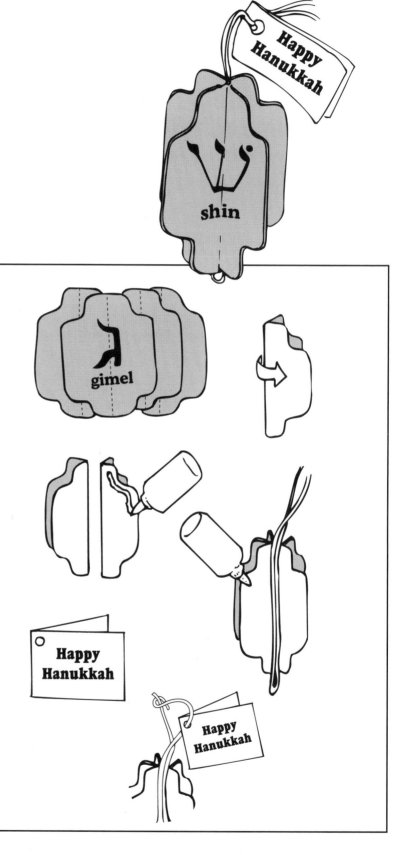

Patterns for hanging dreidel greeting

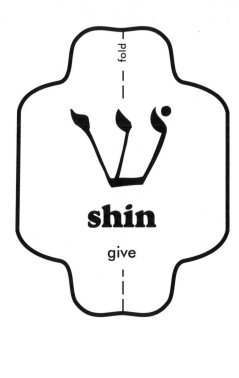

fold

shin

give

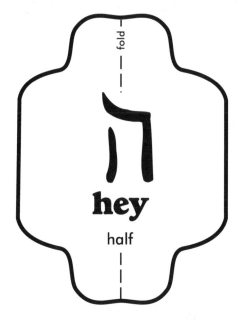

fold

hey

half

fold

gimel

everything

fold

nun

nothing

Happy Hanukkah

Angel Card

Materials:

- patterns (page 19)
- 9" x 12" (23 x 30.5 cm) blue construction paper
- gold foil stars
- glitter
- crayons; scissors; glue

Steps to follow:

1. Color and cut out the angel pattern. Fold the angel in half, open back up, and fold the wings as indicated.

2. Fold the construction paper in half and round the two outside corners.

3. Lay the angel in the blue paper. Make sure the fold of the angel fits securely in the fold of blue paper. Glue the angel in place.

4. Put glue on the angel's halo. Sprinkle with glitter. Let the glue dry completely before closing the card.

5. Add several foil stars around the angel.

6. Close the card. Glue the "Merry Christmas" cloud to the front of the card. Add more foil stars. Glue a seal in place to hold the card shut.

Do not glue the top half of wings.

Optional:

Add a few more gold stars to the outside cover of the card.

Let older students create their own angels to go in the card.

Patterns for angel and cloud

- - - - - - - - - fold - - - - - - - - -

Merry Christmas

How to Make Greeting Cards with Children • EMC 231

Merry Christmas

Materials:

- pattern for tree template (page 21) cut from tagboard
- patterns (page 21)
- 9" x 12" (23 x 30.5 cm) red construction paper
- 4" x 6" (10 x 15 cm) green construction paper
- glitter
- white tempera paint
- pencil with eraser
- crayons; scissors; glue

Steps to follow:

1. Fold the red construction paper in half.

2. Lay the tree template in the center of the card front. Trace around it. Open the card and cut out the tree shape with sharp pointed scissors.

3. Lay the green paper inside the card on the right-hand side. Make sure it fills the cut out tree shape. Glue it in place.

4. Color and cut out the bow pattern. Glue it on top of the green box.

5. Cut out the greeting. Glue it under the box.

6. Dip the pencil eraser in white paint and print round circles on the green paper. Let the paint dry.

7. Close the card. Put a thin line of glue around the outside of the tree. Sprinkle with glitter.

8. Color and cut out the "Merry Christmas" greeting. Glue it to the front of the card.

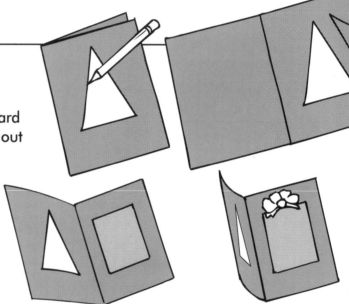

Patterns for tree template, bow, message, and greeting

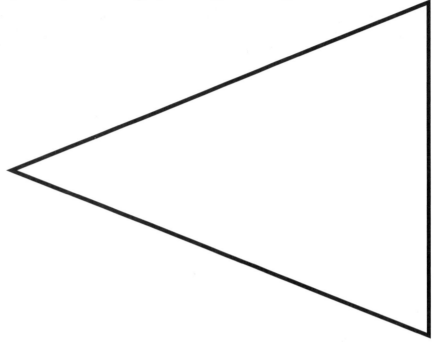

I made this card
And decorated the tree
With Christmas wishes
To you from me.

How to Make Greeting Cards with Children • EMC 231

Oh, Starry Night

Materials:

- patterns (page 23) reproduced on yellow paper
- 6" x 18" (15 x 45.5 cm) blue construction paper
- glitter
- scissors; glue

Steps to follow:

1. Follow these steps to fold the blue paper.

   a. Fold the paper in half.

   b. Open and fold ends to center.

   c. Open and turn over. Bring folds back to center. Crease.

   d. Fold closed on center line.

2. Cut out the stars and greeting panels.

   a. Glue one star on the front cover and one star on the inside back panel.

   b. Glue the remaining two stars on the inside folds so that each star sticks out from its fold.

   c. Cut out and glue the greeting panels in place.

3. On the front of the card make "rays" coming out from the star with glue and glitter.

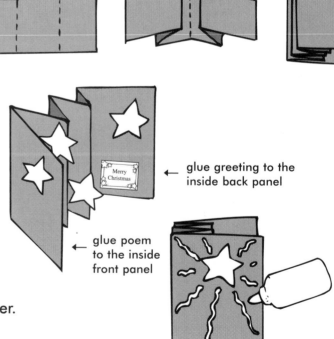

glue greeting to the inside back panel

glue poem to the inside front panel

Optional:

With a black marking pen, draw a small scene of a shepherd and a sheep, a wise man on a camel, or a manger at the bottom of the card.

          How to Make Greeting Cards with Children • EMC 231

Patterns of stars and Christmas messages

Merry Christmas

Each star in the sky

Brings this wish to you,

Merry Christmas and

Happy New Year too!

Christmas Bells

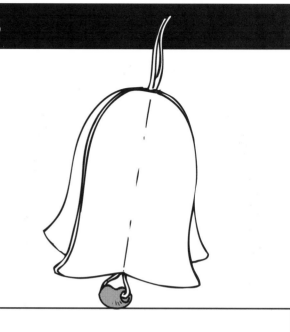

Materials:

- patterns (page 25) reproduced on colored paper
- 18" (45.5 cm) string
- piece of elbow macaroni colored with food coloring mixed with alcohol for quick drying
- scissors; glue
- felt pens

Steps to follow:

1. Cut out the four bells.

2. Fold the bells on the fold line. Press the folded bells firmly.

3. Glue the folded bells together attaching one half of a bell to the next bell. Leave the last section open.

4. Thread the string through the macaroni piece. Tie the ends of the string in a knot. Place the string through the bell with the macaroni at the bottom to form the bell's clapper.

5. Glue the last bell sections together.

6. After the glue has dried, write a Christmas greeting on the bell, putting one word or phrase on each section. For example:

A Very Merry Christmas

I heard the bells on Christmas Day

Ring Out Christmas Joy

Optional:

Use small rubber stamps and stamp pads in Christmas colors to decorate the bells before cutting them out. A bead may be used instead of the elbow macaroni.

Patterns of bells

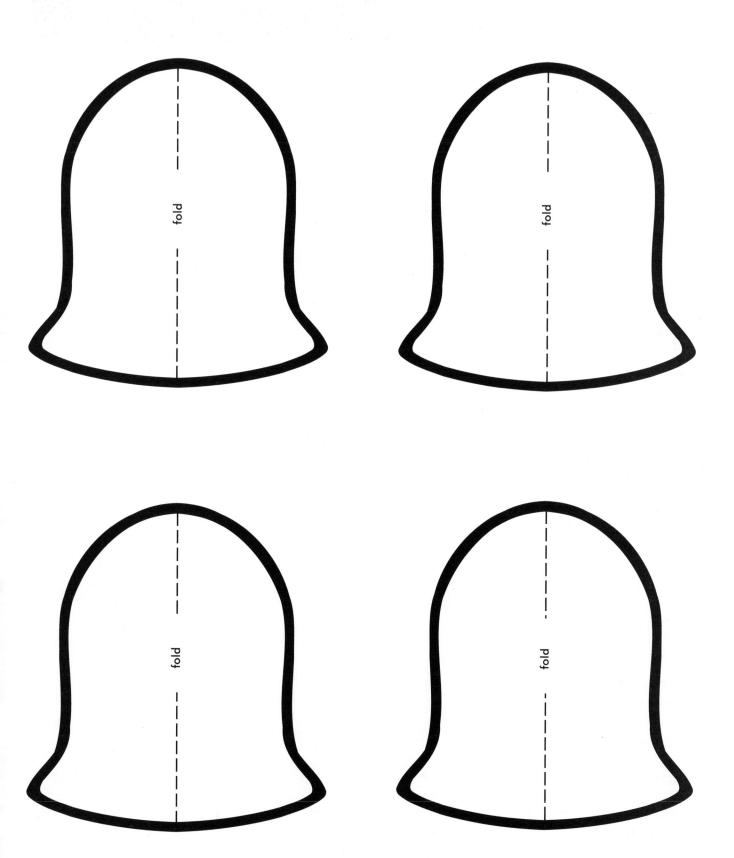

Pop-Up Santa Claus

Materials:

- patterns (page 27)
- 6" x 9" 15 x 23 cm) green construction paper
- crayons or felt marking pens; scissors; glue

Steps to follow:

1. Color the Santa Claus pattern. Write "Merry Christmas" on Santa's banner. Cut the pattern out.

2. Fold the pattern in half and cut along the hat and beard on the gray lines only.

cut beard and hat lines

fold back along side of face

open and refold, pulling santa forward

close and press folds firmly

3. Glue the pop-up inside the construction paper cover.

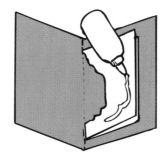
fold construction paper, lay in pop-up, add glue, close, repeat on other side of card

4. Close the card and seal it. Decorate the outside of the card with a border of holly leaves and berries.

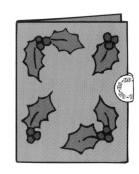

Optional:

Glue white glitter to the beard, moustache, and trim on Santa's hat and gloves, and glue sequins on for eyes to add sparkle.

Pattern for Santa pop-up and seal

Here's My Heart

Materials:

- patterns (page 29)
- 5" x 9" (13 x 23 cm)
  red or pink construction paper
- 18" (45.5 cm) string or narrow ribbon
- scissors; glue
- assorted materials for decorating hearts:
  paint, crayons, felt pens,
  pinking shears, hole punch,
  paper doilies

Steps to follow:

1. Fold the construction paper in half. Lay the large heart pattern along the fold and trace. Cut the heart out, making sure not to cut the folds.

2. Cut out and fold the two small hearts. Glue 1/2 of each heart to the inside of the card as shown. Write a message inside the hearts.

3. Cut out the "Be Mine" heart and glue to the cover. Add additional decorations.

4. Slip the string or ribbon inside the heart and tie in a bow.

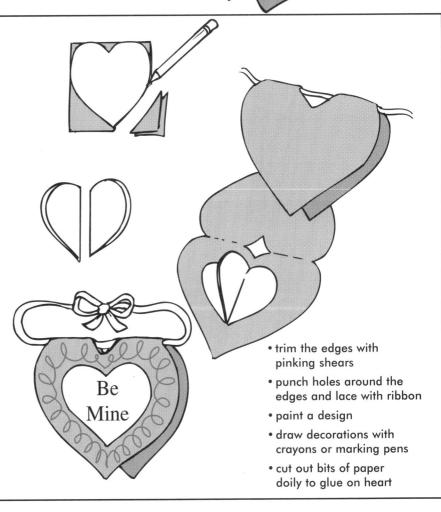

- trim the edges with pinking shears
- punch holes around the edges and lace with ribbon
- paint a design
- draw decorations with crayons or marking pens
- cut out bits of paper doily to glue on heart

Optional:

Cut the heart card from heavy red foil paper. Cut the small hearts from glossy white wrapping paper. Edge with cotton eyelet and use real ribbon. Give this special card to a very special person.

Place top of heart along fold.

Patterns and template for heart card and small hearts

fold

Be Mine

fold

How to Make Greeting Cards with Children • EMC 231

A Valentine Surprise

Materials:

- patterns (page 31)
- 3" x 12" (7.5 x 30.5 cm) red construction paper
- felt pens; pencil; scissors; glue

Steps to follow:

1. Cut out the card pattern. Fold the "flower petals" on fold lines.

2. Decorate both sides of the shape with felt pens. Make small hearts, polka dots, curved lines, etc.

3. Use the heart template to cut several small red hearts to place inside the card. Write a one word message on each heart.

4. Overlap the petals to close the card.

5. Glue on the paper seal to close the card. Write the name of the person the card is meant for on the seal.

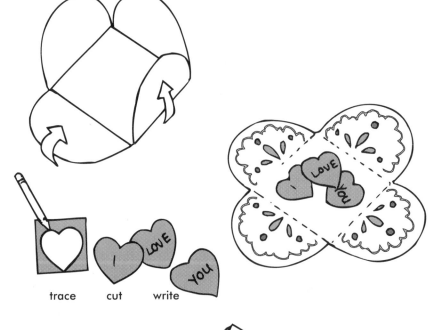

trace   cut   write

Optional:

Use the pattern as a template. Trace it on flowery wrapping paper or bright origami paper. Place heart-shaped confetti inside the Valentine card and seal it with a heart sticker.

Patterns for card, heart, seal

seal

template

How to Make Greeting Cards with Children • EMC 231

It's a Puzzle

Materials:

- puzzle pattern (page 33)
- crayons or felt pens; scissors

Steps to follow:

1. Draw and then color a valentine picture or message on the puzzle pattern.

2. Cut the puzzle apart.

3. Put the puzzle pieces inside an envelope. Give it to a friend.

Optional:

Cut pictures of flowers from magazines. Glue the flowers all over the back of the puzzle pattern. When the glue has dried, write a message such as "A Valentine Bouquet for You" with a black pen somewhere on the flowers. Cut out the puzzle and place in an envelope.

Puzzle Pattern

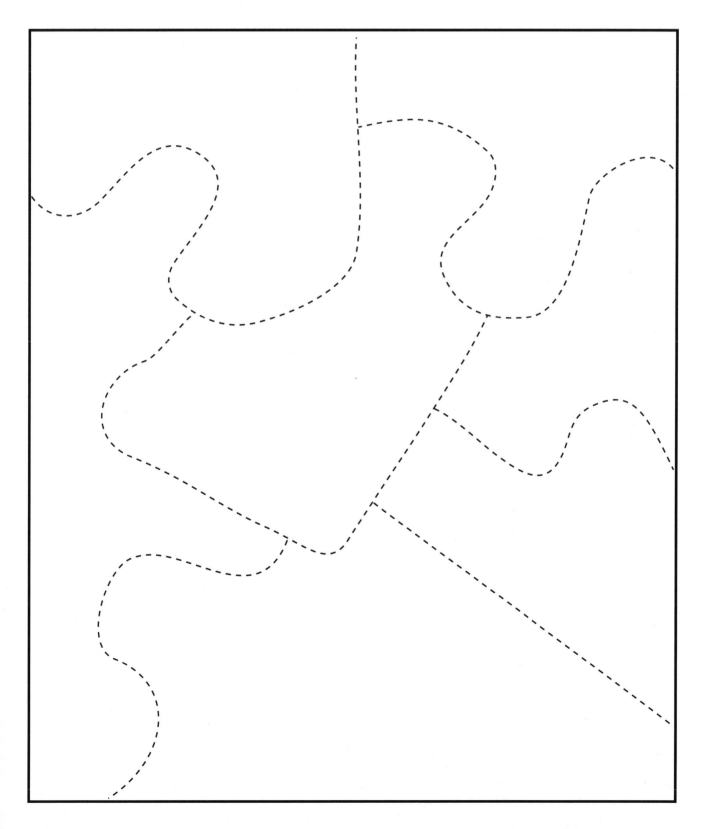

 How to Make Greeting Cards with Children • EMC 231

Swinging Hearts

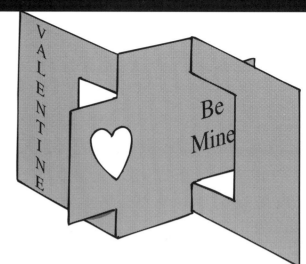

Materials:

- patterns (page 35) reproduced on cardstock
- 4 1/2" x 12" (11.5 x 30.5 cm) red construction paper
- Exacto® Knife (adult use only)
- glue
- marking pens; scissors

Steps to follow:

1. Cut out the card pattern. Make the inside cuts with an Exacto® knife.

2. Fold as shown.

Envelope

1. Fold the red construction paper as shown.

2. Color, cut and fold heart patterns to wrap around sides. Glue in place.

3. Color and cut out the seal. Glue on flap to close envelope.

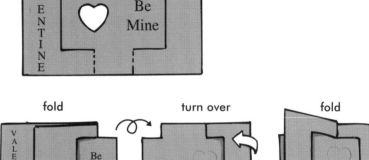

fold   turn over   fold

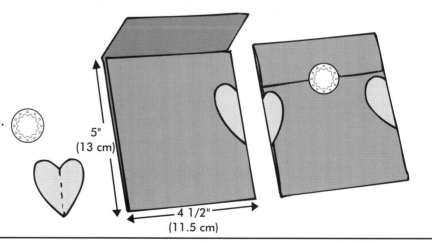

5" (13 cm)

4 1/2" (11.5 cm)

Optional:

Make fancier hearts by cutting with pinking shears or using a special hole punch to punch out tiny hearts. Add paper lace, glitter, sequins, etc.

Patterns for card, envelope hearts, seal

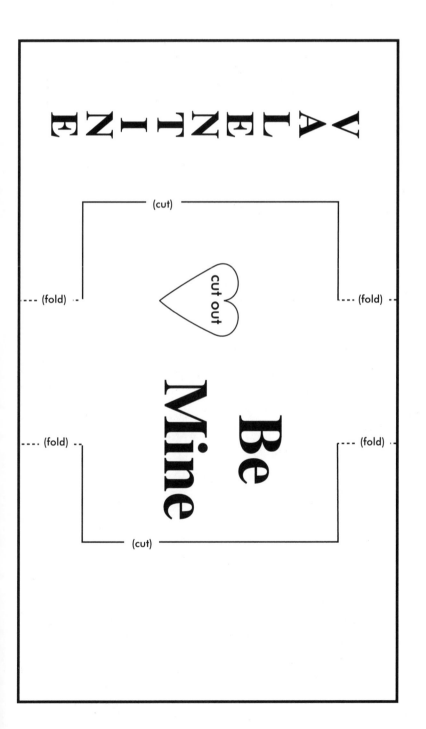

VALENTINE

(cut)

cut out

Be Mine

(fold)   (fold)

(fold)   (fold)

(cut)

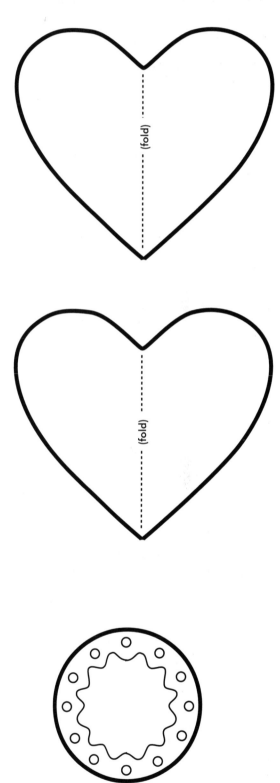

(fold)

(fold)

How to Make Greeting Cards with Children • EMC 231

Hanging Pagoda

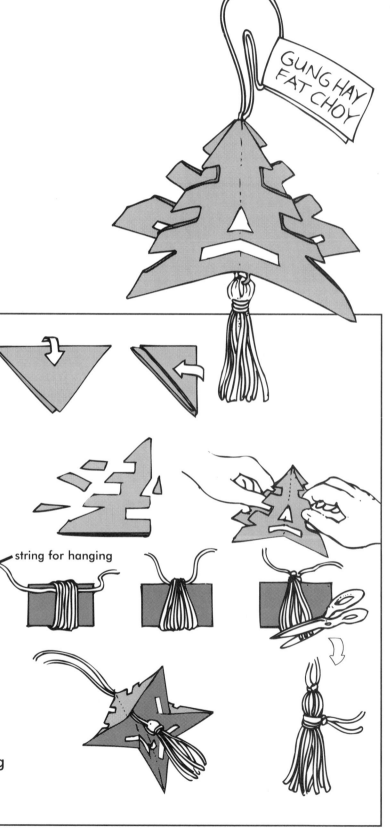

Materials:

- 4 1/4" square of red paper
  (origami or construction)

- 1" x 4" (2.5 x 10 cm)
  white construction paper

- red string or yarn

  12" (30.5 cm) - string for hanging

  6" (15 cm) - to tie tassel

  72" (183 cm) - for tassel

- 3" (7.5 cm) square of cardboard

- pencil; scissors; glue

- marking pen

Steps to follow:

1. Fold the red paper for the pagoda.

2. On the side folds, lightly draw in sections to be cut out. Cut out the sections and open the paper carefully. Refold by pinching in the sides to create the pagoda shape.

3. Make the tassel by wrapping string around cardboard as shown.

4. Poke a hole in the top of the pagoda with a pencil point. Run the string through the hole and tie the ends together.

5. Glue the sides of each point of the pagoda together.

6. Fold white paper in half. Write "Gung Hay Fat Choy" on one side. Glue greeting around the top of the string.

string for hanging

Red Money Pouch

Materials:

- pattern (page 38)
  reproduced on red paper
- a small coin
- cellophane tape
- scissors
- gold seal

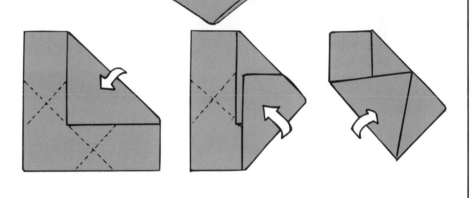

Steps to follow:

1. Cut out the pattern.
Fold on marked lines in
the order numbered.

2. Open flap 4 and insert
the small coin.

3. Close flap 4 with a
piece of tape.

4. Secure the pouch with
a gold seal.

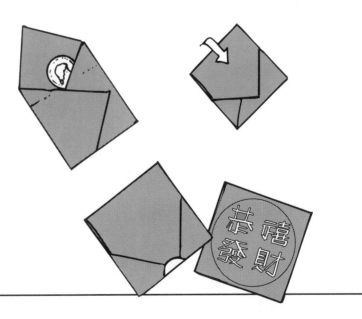

Optional:

Use the pattern as a template and cut the pouch from red origami paper. Secure the pocket
with a gold seal.

Pattern for money pouch

The Chinese characters
say Gung Hay Fat Choy

The Chinese characters
say Gung Hay Fat Choy

"Hoppy" St. Patrick's Day

Materials:

- patterns (page 40)
- 6 1/2" x 12" (17 x 30.5 cm) white construction paper
- green tempera paint in a shallow dish
- shamrock shaped stamp (from sponge or potato or purchased stamp)
- crayons; scissors; glue

Steps to follow:

1. Fold construction paper in half. Open and lay flat. Print with shamrock print stamp. Let dry while the rest of the card is prepared.

2. Color the frog and shamrock seal green. Cut out and fold as indicated.

3. Glue the frog inside the card. Glue the frogs head on top of the body as shown. Lift the flap and write a message.

4. Glue the shamrock seal in place to close the card.

Shamrock Stamp

Cut a shamrock shape in half a potato or cut one out of a sponge.

Pattern for frog and shamrock seal

fold

"Hoppy"
St. Patrick's Day!

Easter Surprise

Materials:

- pattern (page 42)
  reproduced on pastel construction paper
- 8" x 9" (20 x 23 cm)
  construction paper—spring colors
- Exacto® knife (adult use only)
- felt pens; scissors; glue

Steps to follow:

1. Color and cut out the pattern pieces. One egg will glue to the card, two eggs will be used to seal envelope.

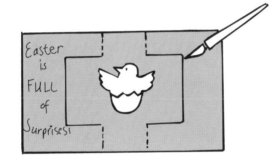

2. Use an Exacto® knife to cut on solid lines only.

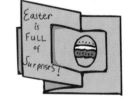

3. Fold on dotted lines. First fold right side in. Flip the card over and fold right side in again.

4. Glue one of the eggs onto the swinging flap. Write "Easter is full of surprises!" on left hand panel.

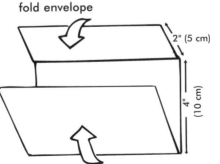

fold envelope

2" (5 cm)

4" (10 cm)

glue seals in place

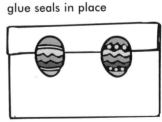

Optional:

Cover up the hatching chick before reproducing the pattern. Have students create their own surprise to go on each side of the swinging door.

Patterns for card and eggs

Easter Bunny

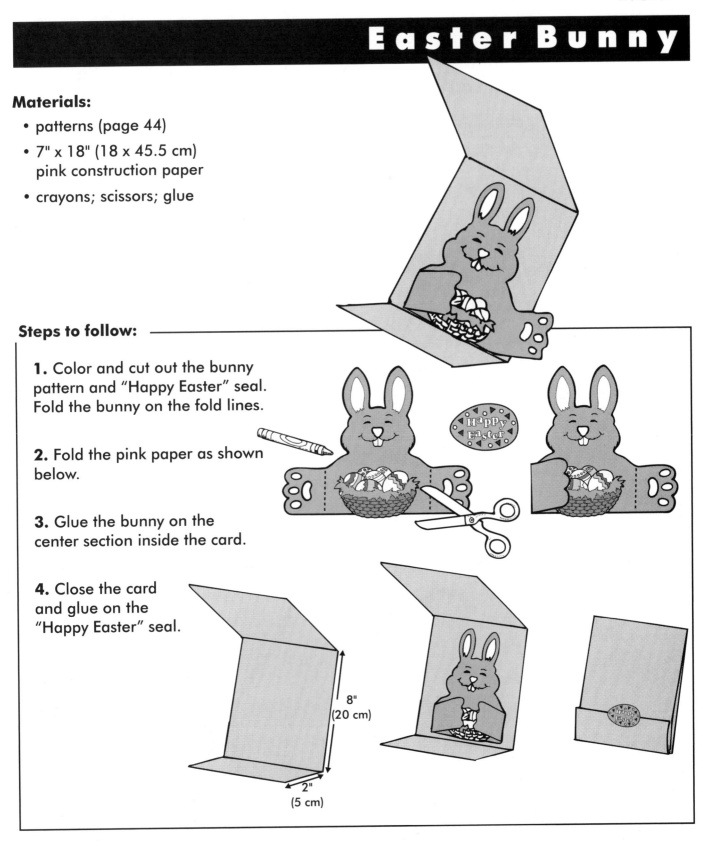

Materials:

- patterns (page 44)
- 7" x 18" (18 x 45.5 cm) pink construction paper
- crayons; scissors; glue

Steps to follow:

1. Color and cut out the bunny pattern and "Happy Easter" seal. Fold the bunny on the fold lines.

2. Fold the pink paper as shown below.

3. Glue the bunny on the center section inside the card.

4. Close the card and glue on the "Happy Easter" seal.

8" (20 cm)

2" (5 cm)

Optional:

Use watercolors to complete the card. Paint a border, a swirling design, spring flowers, or Easter eggs on the outside of the card in spring colors.

43

A Basket of Easter Surprises

Materials:

- pattern (page 46)
- 8" x 8" (20 x 20 cm) yellow construction paper
- 6" x 9" (15 x 23 cm) white construction paper
- 18" (45.5 cm) ribbon or yarn
- crayons or felt pens; scissors; glue

Steps to follow:

1. Color and cut out the basket pattern. Cut the inside of the handle out carefully so as not to cut the egg template. Fold on the lines. Glue the sides closed.

2. Tie the ribbon to the handle of the basket. Then glue the basket to the yellow construction paper.

3. Use the egg pattern as a template. Trace eggs on the white construction paper. Decorate the eggs with crayons or felt pens and then cut them out. Put the eggs into the basket.

Optional:

Write Easter messages on the reverse side of each egg.

Cut the eggs out of tagboard and decorate them:

   a. Paint designs with watercolors.

   b. Glue on bits of ribbon and lace. Add buttons, sequins, and other small objects.

   c. Print patterns with small rubber stamps.

Patterns for basket and eggs

A Basket Full of Surprises!

fold

egg template

May Basket

Materials:

- patterns (page 48)
- construction paper scraps —assorted colors
- 9" x 18" (23 x 45.5 cm) piece of string or ribbon
- hole punch
- pencil
- crayons; scissors; glue

Steps to follow:

1. Trace around the basket pattern and fold on the lines.

2. Punch holes where indicated.

3. Create paper flowers from the colored paper scraps. Glue them in place.

4. Write a message inside the basket. Fold the sides of the card toward the middle. Glue the "Happy May Day" seal in place to close the card.

5. Punch a hole in the top. Insert the string or ribbon through the hole. Tie a knot and then a bow. Surprise a friend with the basket card on May Day.

Optional:

Create flowers for the basket in other ways:

    a. Use flower stickers for flowers.

    b. Use flower rubber stamps and brightly colored stamp pads.

    c. Dry real flowers and glue to basket.

    d. Cut flowers out of magazines.

Patterns for basket and Happy May Day seal

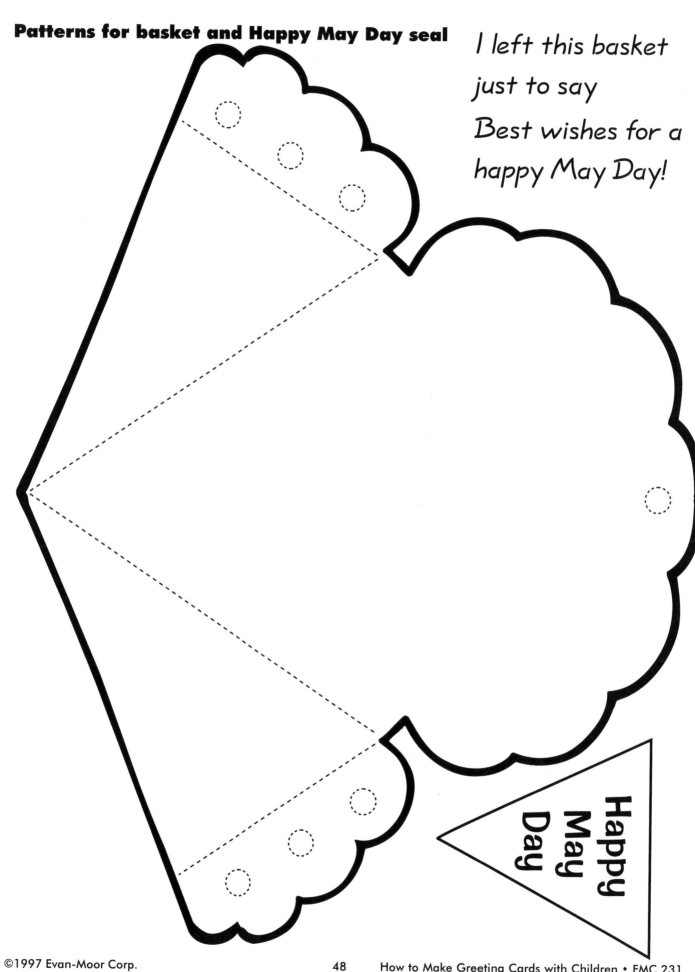

I left this basket
just to say
Best wishes for a
happy May Day!

Happy
May
Day

 How to Make Greeting Cards with Children • EMC 231

Butterfly Card

Materials:

- pattern (page 50)
- 6" x 10" (15 x 25.5 cm) construction paper—any color
- scraps of black construction paper
- decoration choices—crayons, felt pens, colored pencils, water colors
- scissors; glue

Steps to follow:

1. Color the butterfly pattern.

2. Fold and cut as shown.

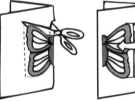

3. Cut antennae from black scraps. Glue to the butterfly's head.

4. Glue the pop-up inside the construction paper cover.

5. Decorate the outside of the card in the same medium used to color the butterfly. Close the card and seal with a pretty sticker.

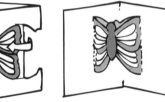

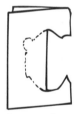

cut top and lower portion of wings on gray lines

fold back at side of wing

open and pull butterfly forward

close and press folds

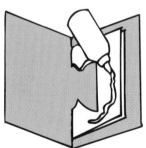

Fold construction paper.

Lay pop-up pattern against the fold. Put glue on pop-up, close the cover and press. Repeat on other side.

Optional:

Make torn paper butterflies to decorate the outside of the card. Close with a butterfly sticker.

Pattern for pop-up butterfly

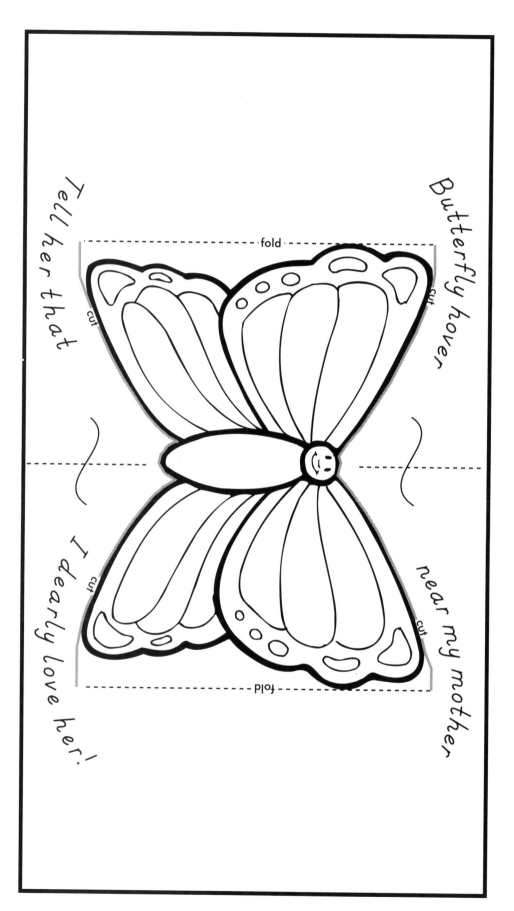

Tell her that

I dearly love her!

Butterfly hover

near my mother

fold

fold

cut

cut

cut

cut

How to Make Greeting Cards with Children • EMC 231

A Spiral Greeting

Materials:

- patterns (page 52)
- 9" x 12" (23 x 30.5 cm) construction paper
- 18" (45.4 cm) piece of string
- hole punch
- felt marking pens; scissors; glue

Steps to follow:

1. Use marking pens to write a message to Mom on the spiral starting in the center.

- *Dear Mom, I love you very much.*
- *Dear Mother, Thank you for everything you do for me.*
- *Dear Mom, You're the greatest!*

2. Cut out the spiral circle (outside only) and "Mom" tag. Glue them to the construction paper. Let the glue dry.

3. Cut out the spiral circle. Continue cutting along the inner line.

4. Punch a hole in the center of the spiral.

5. Cut out the "Mom" tag leaving an edge of colored paper all the way around. Fold in half and punch a hole as marked.

6. Put the string through the hole in the spiral and in the card. Tie the ends of the string in a knot.

Optional:

Decorate the back side of the spiral with a design of stripes and/or dots using felt pens. Or print a design using small rubber stamps and stamp pads.

Pattern for spiral and "Mom" tag

Mom

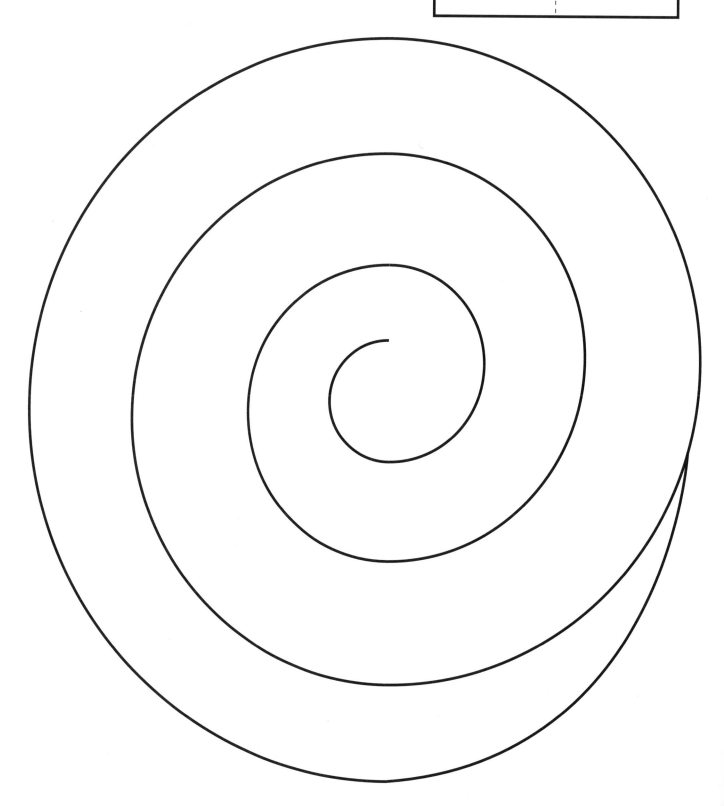

Kitty Card

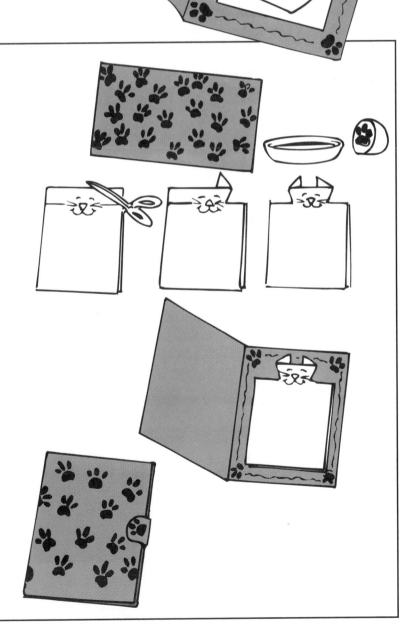

Materials:

- patterns (page 54)
- 7" x 12" (18 x 30.5 cm) construction paper—bright color
- kitty paw print potato stamp (see below)
- black tempera paint in shallow container
- felt marking pens; scissors; glue

Steps to follow:

1. Fold construction paper in half. Open and lay flat. Print with paw print stamp. Let dry while the rest of the card is prepared.

2. Color and cut out the kitty pattern. Fold and cut as indicated.

3. Glue the kitty inside the card. Lift the flap and write a message to Mother. (Have a "purrrfect" day!) Add more kitty paw prints at each corner to frame the kitty. Let the paint dry.

4. Close the card with the paw seal.

**Pattern for kitty and
paw print seal**

fold

cut   cut

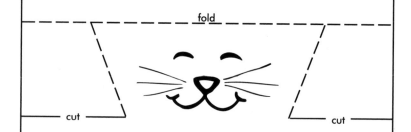

My Dad

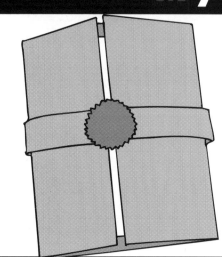

Materials:

- pattern (page 56)
- 9" x 12" (23 x 30.5 cm) construction paper—any color
- crayons; scissors; glue; felt pens; pinking shears
- 2 1/2" (6.5 cm) square pieces of construction paper

Steps to follow:

1. Cut a 2" (5 cm) strip off the construction paper.

2. Fold the edges of the larger piece of construction paper to meet at the center.

3. Cut out the pattern pieces.

   a. Color or make a pattern along the edge of the frame. Draw a picture of Dad in the center of the frame.

   b. Complete the sentence "Dad, you are special to me because…"

   c. Draw a line or put dots around the edge of the poem.

4. Glue the completed pattern pieces inside the card.

5. Close the card. Wrap the long construction paper strip around the card. Fasten the strip with a seal cut with pinking shears from the square piece of construction paper.

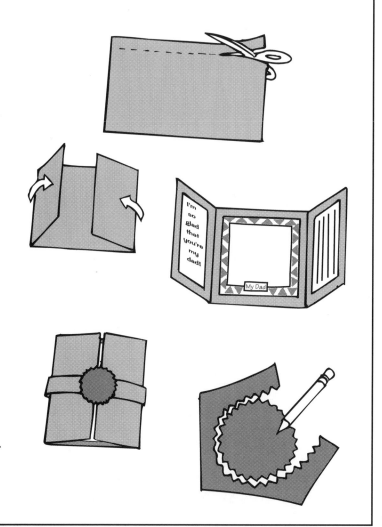

Optional:

Have students replace the poem with a picture of something their fathers enjoy doing or symbols of their occupations (fish for a fisherman, tools for a carpenter, etc.).

Patterns for frame, poem, and message

_____

_____

_____

_____

Dad, you are special to me because

cut

My Dad

cut

I'm

so

glad

that

you're

my

dad!

Shadow Box

Materials:

- pattern (page 58)
- 18" (45.5 cm) narrow ribbon
- felt pens; crayons
- pencil

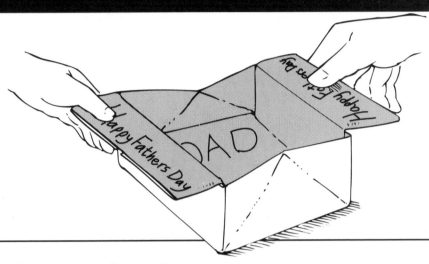

Steps to follow:

1. Use felt pens or crayons to make a design all over the pattern page.

2. Fold the pattern as shown. Crease each fold well.

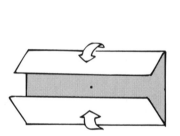

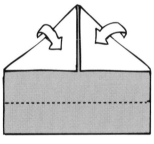

c. Fold both line 4's in to meet.

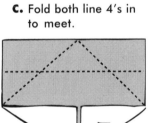

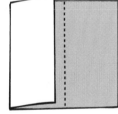

a. Fold lines 1 & 2 to center dot.

b. Fold both line 3's in to meet.

d. Fold in on lines 5 & 6.

e. Open all folds. Refold lines 1 & 2. Orient paper so that line 6 is away from you. Lift up end, letting it fold on line 6. Pull right corner open and crease line 3 from center dot to corner. Repeat on left side, creasing line 4 from center dot to corner.

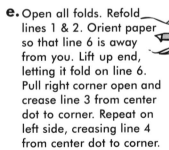

f. Pull end of box toward you and press flat.

g. Fold in wings.

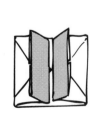

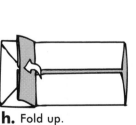

h. Fold up.

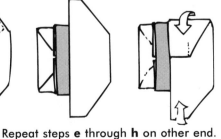

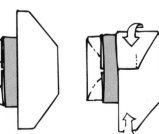

Repeat steps **e** through **h** on other end.

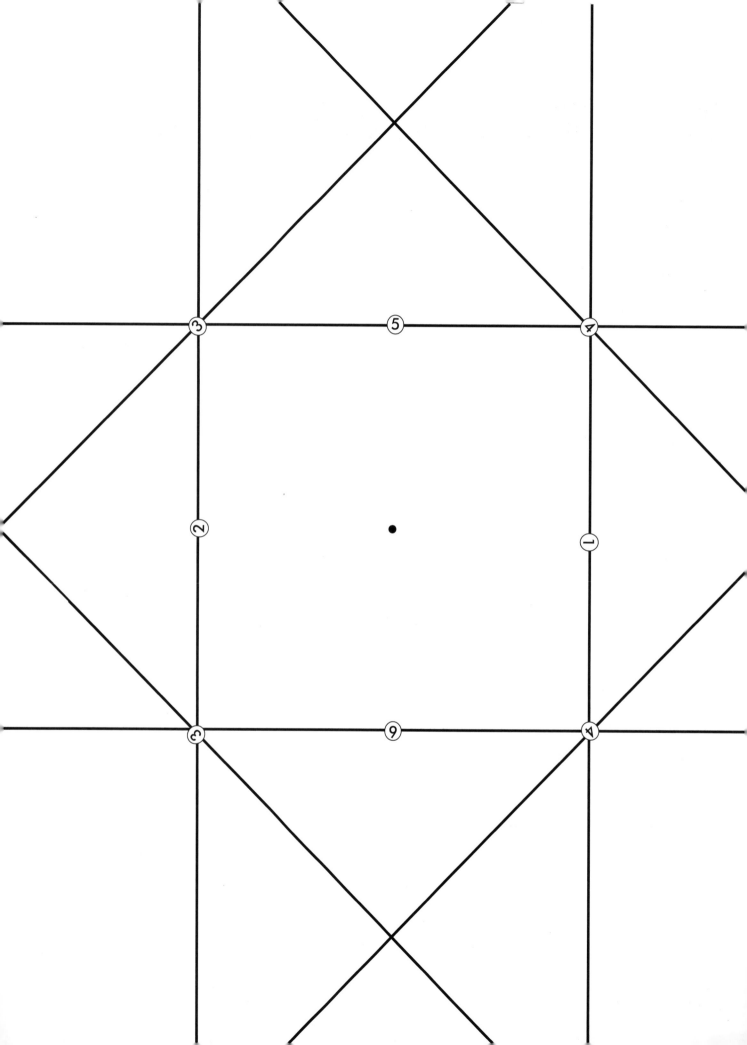

Father's Shirt Card

Materials:

- patterns (page 60)
- 7" x 12" (18 x 30.5 cm) construction paper—any color
- assorted colors of construction paper scraps
- crayons; scissors; glue

Steps to follow:

1. Cut out the pattern pieces.

2. Fold and cut the shirt as shown.

3. Color the shirt to resemble one Father might like.

4. Write a greeting or message to Father inside the shirt.

5. Fold the construction paper in half. Glue the shirt and the poem inside the card.

6. Close the card and secure it with the button seal.

7. Cut bowties from construction paper to decorate front of card.

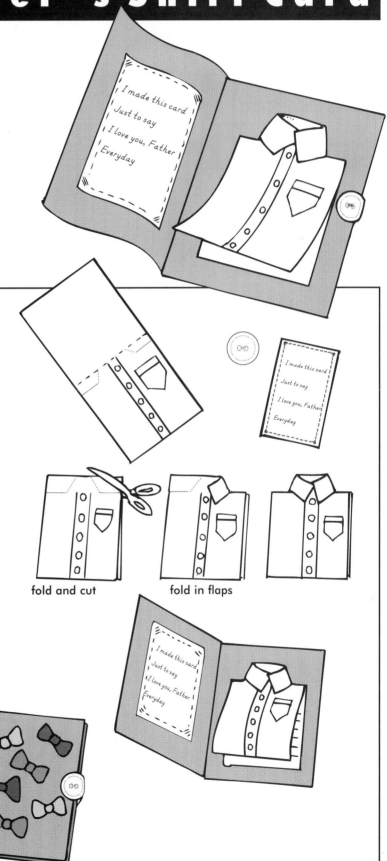

fold and cut   fold in flaps

Pattern for shirt and message

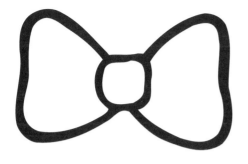

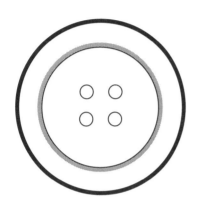

I made this card

Just to say

I love you, Father

Everyday

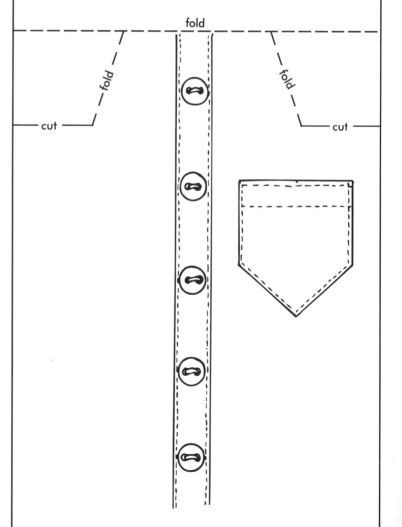

Thank You Spiral

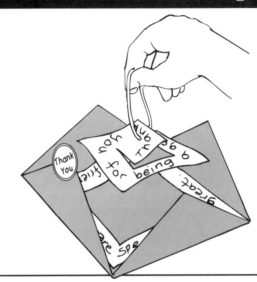

Materials:

- pattern (page 62)
- 9" (23 cm) square construction paper—any color
- 12" (30.5 cm) piece of string
- hole punch
- felt marking pens; scissors; pencil; glue

Steps to follow:

1. Cut out the patterns. Write a thank you message along the spiral starting in the center. Then cut on the line.

2. Punch a hole in the center. Put the string through the hole and tie the ends in a knot.

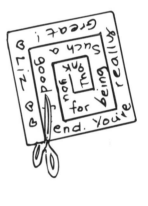

3. Fold the construction paper as shown to make an envelope.

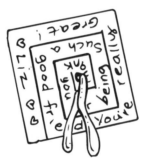

4. Open the envelope and lay the spiral inside. Refold and secure with a seal.

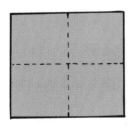

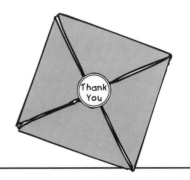

Optional:

Decorate the back side of the spiral with felt markers before cutting it out. Make a simple border on the envelope.

Pattern for spiral and seal

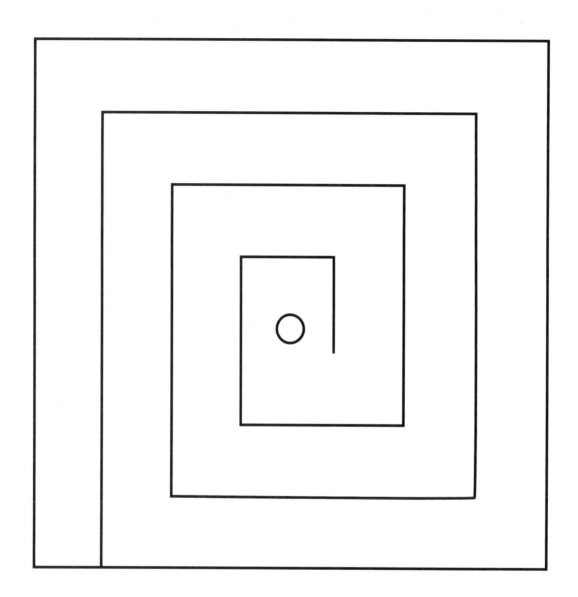

How to Make Greeting Cards with Children • EMC 231

YOU're So Nice

Materials:

- pattern (page 64) reproduced on card stock or construction paper
- Exacto® knife (adult use only)
- 8" (20 cm) piece of ribbon
- small self-closing plastic bag
- hole punch
- crayons; scissors

Steps to follow:

1. Cut out the pattern. Cut the inside lines with an Exacto® knife.

2. Fold on the lines.

3. Write "Thank You" on the front. Then pull card open and it says "You're So Nice."

4. Decorate the outside frame with a border design.

5. Put the finished card into a plastic bag. Punch a hole in the corner of the plastic bag. Fold ribbon in half and push the loop through the hole. Pull the ends through the loop and tie a knot at the end.

Optional:

Use stick-on dots, colorful stickers, or permanent felt markers to decorate the plastic bag.

Pattern for card

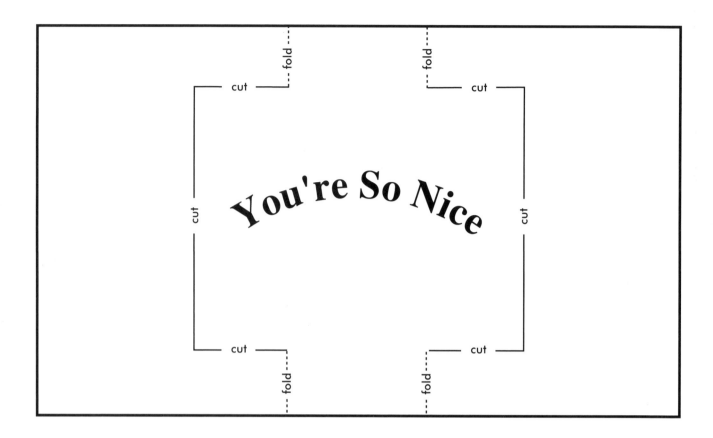

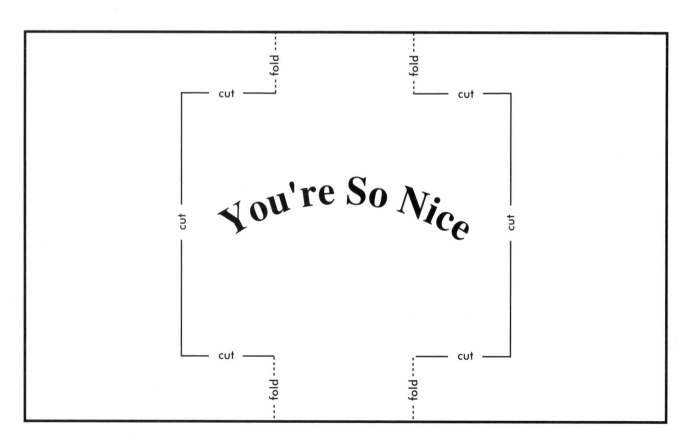

Pop-Up Puppy

Materials:

- patterns (page 66)
- 9" X 12" (23 x 30.5 cm) construction paper—any color
- felt marking pens; scissors; glue

Steps to follow:

1. Color and cut out all of the dog pattern pieces. Fold as marked.

2. Fold the construction paper in half. Lay the dog inside as shown.

3. Apply glue to one tab on the dog. Close the card. Flip the card over and apply glue to the other tab. Close the card and press.

4. Glue the "Get Well" message and the poem inside the card.

5. Secure the card with the bone seal.

Optional:

Draw or cut small paper bones to make a border around the edge of the card.

Have students write their own "get well" poems or messages to put inside the card.

Pattern for dog, poem, and get well message

I know it's terrible

To feel so sick.

Puppy brings my wishes

that you'll get well quick.

Bow Wow

Puppet Friends

Materials:

- patterns (pages 68 and 69)
- 4 1/2" x 12" (12 x 30.5 cm) construction paper—any color
- Exacto® knife (adult use only)
- cellophane tape
- crayons; scissors; glue

Steps to follow:

1. Color and cut out the finger puppet patterns.

2. Fold on lines and glue the back flaps of the puppets together.

3. Fold the envelope in thirds. Cut the corners off the top flap. Fold flap down and make a mark with a pencil on both sides of the flap, about 1 1/2" (4 cm) up from the bottom. Open again and use an Exacto® knife to make a slit. Tape sides together.

4. Put puppets inside envelope.

1½" (4 cm)

Patterns for puppets

 How to Make Greeting Cards with Children • EMC 231

How to Make Greeting Cards with Children • EMC 231

Birthday Greetings

A Long Birthday Wish

Materials:

- patterns (page 71)
- 2" x 18" (5 x 45.5 cm) white construction paper
- 6" x 9" (15 x 23 cm) construction paper—any color
- crayons; scissors; glue; felt pens

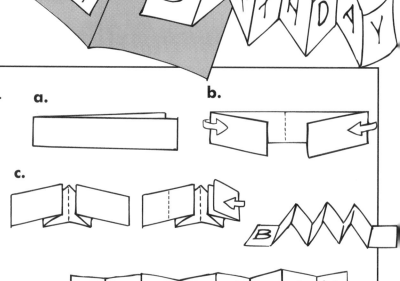

Steps to follow:

1. Accordion fold the long strip of paper.
   a. Fold strip in half.
   b. Open and fold ends to center.
   c. Flip over and bring folds to center.
   d. Fold ends to center and crease.

2. Write one letter of the word "birthday" in each section of the accordion strip. It's important that you begin on the correct section so that the greeting pulls out. (See illustration.)

3. Color and cut out the letters "Happy" and the cupcake.

4. Fold the colored paper in half. Glue the letters "Happy" on the left side. Paste the accordion strip on the right side of the card so that the "B" is pasted down. Glue the cupcake on top. Draw in the correct number of candles to show how old the birthday person is.

5. Close the card. Decorate the outside with colorful balloons and secure it with the balloon seal or a sticker.

Optional:

Instead of balloons, cut out a party hat and noise maker from bits of bright construction paper to glue on the outside of the card. Tear bits of paper, and then glue them around the card to look like thrown confetti.

Patterns for "HAPPY", cupcake, and seal

Birthday Greetings

Pop-Up Birthday Cake

Materials:

- patterns (page 73)
- 6" x 9" (15 x 23 cm) construction paper—any color
- 2 10" (25.5 cm) pieces of narrow ribbon
- hole punch
- crayons; scissors; glue

Steps to follow:

1. Color and cut out all pattern pieces.

2. Make the pop-up form.
- a. Fold form in half and cut tab.
- b. Fold and crease tab in both directions.
- c. Open form and pull tab forward.

3. Color and cut any number of candles and add to the cake. Glue cake to tab. Write a birthday message.

4. Fold the construction paper in half.

5. Lay the folded pop-up in the folder. Apply glue to the top side of the pop-up. (Be sure the fold of the pop-up is up against the fold of the card.) Close the card and press. Flip card over and glue other side of pop-up.

6. Punch a hole at the bottom and the top of the card. Tie a ribbon to each hole. Close the card by tying the ribbons in a bow.

Optional:

Glue a sprinkling of glitter to the tip of each candle flame.

Use watercolors to paint a design to the outside of the card.

Patterns for pop-up form, cake, and candles

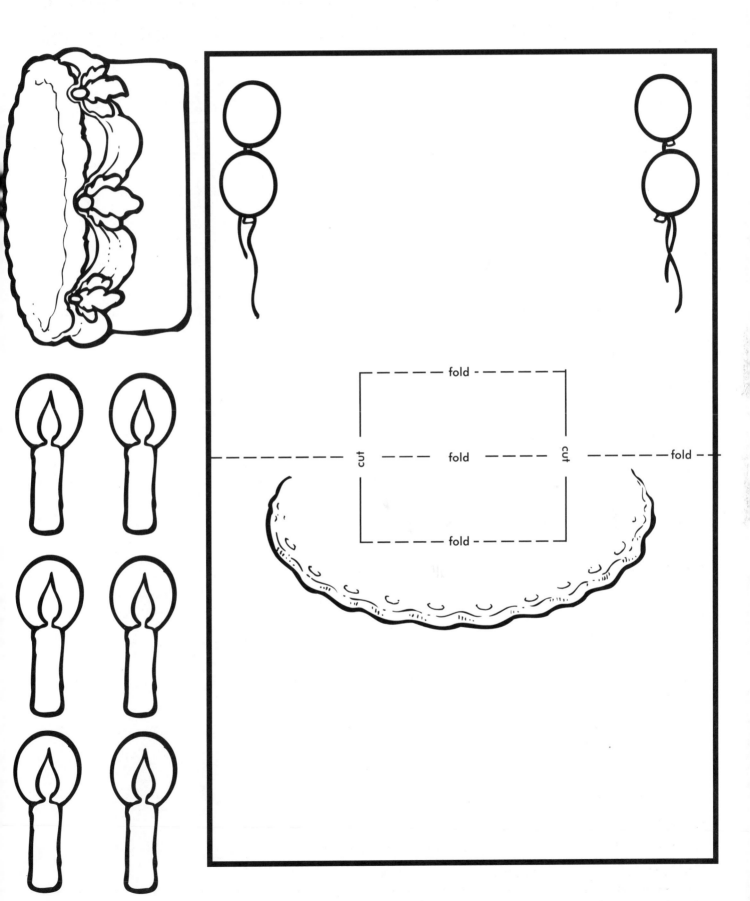

Invitation

Open House Invitation

Materials:

- patterns (page 75)
- 6" x 12" (15 x 30.5 cm) green construction paper
- crayons; scissors; glue

Steps to follow:

1. Color and cut out all pattern pieces. Fold the house on the lines.

2. Fold the construction paper in half. Open and lay flat. Glue both flaps of the schoolhouse inside.

3. Glue the "playground" and the invitation to the card.

4. Glue on the "Please Come" seal to close the card.

5. Decorate the outside of the card with stick-on stars.

Patterns for invitation form and seal

You're Invited

Where: _____

_____

_____

When: _____

_____

Please Come

You're Invited

Where: _____

_____

_____

When: _____

_____

Please Come

Envelopes

If a card is to go through the mail, keep any envelope decorations to a minimum—a simple border, one small sketch in the lower, left-hand corner, etc. This will leave room for clear addresses, and a stamp.

Self-Closing:

Many of the cards in this book do not need an envelope. The outside of the card can be closed with a ribbon, sticker, seal, etc. to protect the design and message inside.

Ready-Made:

Envelopes can be purchased at stationery stores or discount office supply warehouses. Report card envelopes can be used for larger cards. Self-closing plastic bags can be used with puzzle cards and spiral cards. Small colorful sacks can be used to carry hanging cards.

Decorate the outside of these envelopes, plastic bags, or sacks using the same decoration techniques used on the card.

Make Your Own Envelopes:

The size paper needed for the envelope will depend on the width and length of the finished card.

Envelope # 1

Start with a rectangular sheet of paper. Fold the paper in thirds. Unfold and round the top corners. Fold up bottom piece and glue sides.

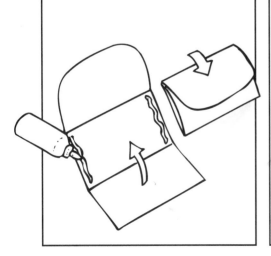

Envelope # 2

Draw a rectangle in the middle of your paper (1). Draw another rectangle the same size below the first rectangle (2). Draw side and top flaps as shown and round corners. Fold sides in and apply glue. Fold bottom flap up.

Envelope # 3

Draw a square in the middle of your paper (1). Draw a second square the same size below the first (2). Draw triangles projecting from 3 sides of the top square. Cut out the pattern. Fold bottom flap up first. Apply glue to outside edges of two side flaps. Fold each one in. Fold top flap down and seal closed.

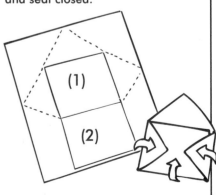

Decorating Techniques

There are endless ideas when it comes to decorating greeting cards; however, it is often best not to "overdecorate." Keeping the design simple will help show off the card and keep the focus on the greeting rather than the artwork. Don't forget the envelope! Adding a simple splash of color, a rubber stamp, or piece of colored paper to the envelope helps to complete the handmade greeting.

Printing

Look all around you; there are many kinds of everyday objects that you can use to print with.

- rubber stamp
- sponge
- potato
- finger
- leaf
- cork
- pencil eraser

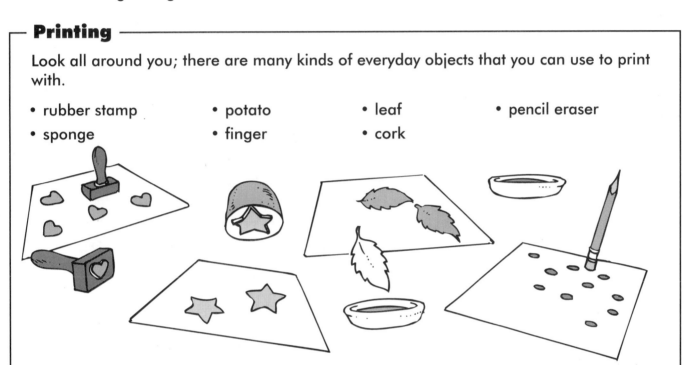

Paint

- spatter with toothbrush
- watercolor
- batik effect (watercolor over crayon)
- fork/comb dragging
- feathering (dribble paint on paper, lay another piece of paper over it and rub, then lift off)

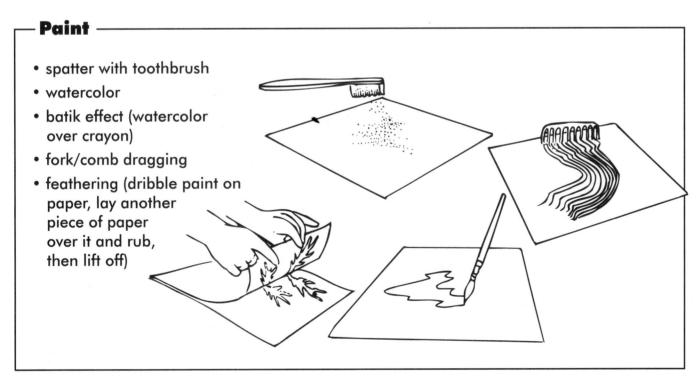

Stenciling

Stenciling can provide a variety of effects and can turn a very simple design into a complex pattern. Used cereal boxes provide a nice weight cardboard that is easily cut and withstands repeated use.

- colored pencil
- paint with sponge
- crayon: color the design, then watercolor over entire project for batik effect
- soft pastels: rub pastels onto another sheet of paper to create a powder. Use a cotton swab or cosmetic sponge to apply.

Paper

- decorate torn pieces of brown paper bags
- assorted torn paper
- paper collage
- designs cut from wrapping paper
- crepe paper bows
- woven strips

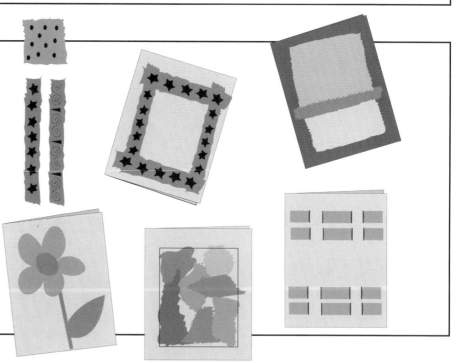

Addressing envelopes
Carry the same design and color theme over from the card to the envelope.

Seals
Try all different shapes, including initials, or cut out a section of design from wrapping paper and glue it to a piece of heavier paper.